Factories
in Space

Today's World in Space

Factories
in Space

By David Baker

Rourke Enterprises, Inc.
Vero Beach, FL 32964

Library of Congress Cataloging-in-Publication Data

Baker, David, 1944-
  Factories in space.

  (Today's world in space)
  Bibliography: p.
  Includes index.
  Summary: Focuses on NASA's plans to design a permanently manned space station in the mid 1990's which would enable scientists to explore and colonize the moon.
    1. Space stations—Juvenile literature. 2. Space industrialization—Juvenile literature. [1. Space stations. 2. Space industrialization] I. Title. II. Series.
TL797.B35 1987   629.44'2   87-16689
ISBN O-86592-409-0

CONTENTS

Skylab
Shows
the Way

When the first United States astronauts went into space, they were in small capsules with very little room to move around. The first, Mercury, carried one pilot in a cramped spacecraft 6 feet wide and 11 feet tall. At launch, Mercury weighed less than 4,300 pounds. Six astronauts went into space in Mercury capsules. In 1961, two astronauts made *ballistic* flights 118 miles into space before falling straight back to the sea. These flights proved that manned space flight was possible. In 1962 and 1963, four orbital flights were made using Mercury capsules. The last flight remained in space for 34 hours, and the spacecraft made 22 orbits of the earth.

In May 1961, nine months before the first manned orbital flight by an American, President John F. Kennedy made it a national goal for two

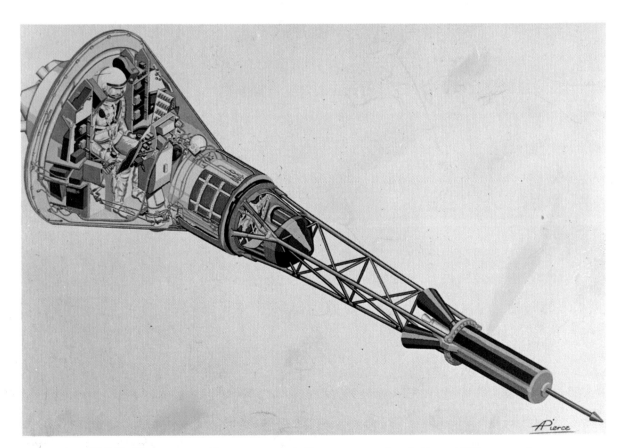

NASA's tiny one-man Mercury spacecraft was cramped and allowed little space for the pilot to move around.

carry two astronauts on flights lasting up to 14 days, practice linking up in space with a target vehicle, and show how astronauts could leave their capsule and drift around in a spacesuit. The 10 flights were a great success and helped prepare the way for Apollo.

Apollo flights began in 1968 and led soon to a manned landing on the moon in July, 1969. The Apollo spacecraft was 33 feet long, 12 feet 10 inches in diameter and weighed almost 33 tons. The *lunar module* that carried men to the lunar surface was a spider-like vehicle 23 feet tall and 31 feet across the landing legs. It weighed up to 18 tons. Docked together for the long flight to the moon, the Apollo and the lander stretched 64 feet and their combined weight was more than 50 tons. Each Apollo and lander weighed more than all 10 manned Gemini spacecraft combined.

Above: NASA launched ten manned Gemini missions in 1965 and 1966 to practice the many different techniques needed to land men on the moon.

Below: The Apollo spacecraft was built to ferry astronauts from the surface of the earth to moon orbit, where a two-man lander would carry astronauts to the lunar surface.

astronauts to land on the moon by the end of the 1960s. To achieve this required massive amounts of work by scientists, engineers, and others involved in the space program. They came up with Apollo, designed to carry three men into orbit. From there, a lander would carry two astronauts to the surface. To test important steps essential to Apollo's success, a modified version of Mercury was built for 10 manned missions in 1965 and 1966.

Called Gemini, the new spacecraft was much bigger than Mercury. Gemini was 19 feet long, including a special adapter with a maximum diameter of 10 feet. The complete spacecraft weighed about 7,500 pounds. Gemini would

Saturn V, the giant rocket that sent Apollo to the moon, was twenty times more powerful than the rocket used to put Mercury into orbit. Saturn V had three stages. The first used kerosene and liquid oxygen to push the upper stages and Apollo to a speed of about 5,200 MPH. It separated, fell away into the sea and left the second stage to push the rest to a speed of 14,300 MPH. That too fell away, leaving the third stage to provide the thrust to get into orbit at 17,500 MPH. The third stage was used again on the second orbit to push Apollo toward the moon, adding an extra 7,000 MPH.

Both the second and third Saturn V stages used liquid hydrogen and liquid oxygen. Each stage was in fact two separate tanks divided inside by a common bulkhead. In each stage, the hydrogen tank was much bigger than the oxygen tank. Engineers studied ways of using the third stage in orbit. Instead of carrying Apollo and boosting it to the moon, the empty third stage could be fitted out as a *space station*. Engineers then realized that the first two stages of Saturn V could lift an empty third fitted out on the ground for habitation by visiting astronauts.

Skylab was a converted third stage of the Saturn V launch vehicle, equipped with additional laboratory work space and six large solar cell panels for electrical power.

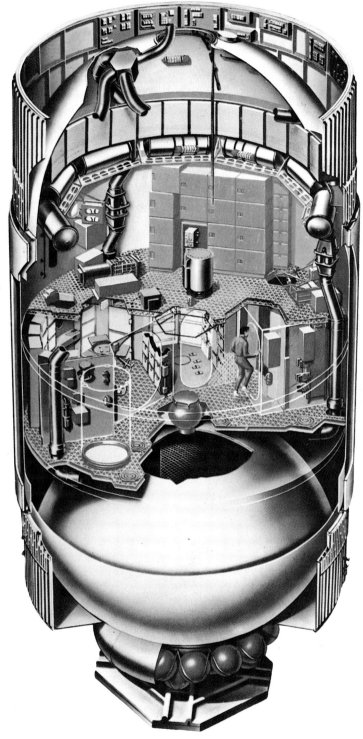

The converted liquid hydrogen tank of the Saturn V rocket stage allowed plenty of room for astronauts testing scientific equipment and experiments.

Called Skylab, the makeshift space station was more than a modified Saturn V third stage. It was a laboratory completely fitted out with work areas, living quarters, medical experiments, and much scientific equipment. Two extra modules on top provided an airlock so astronauts could make observations of the earth and carry out welding tests. A huge array of telescopes for observing the sun was fixed to an enormous hinged cage on top. Once in orbit, the telescope structure was moved around to the side, leaving a docking hatch clear in front. Manned visits would be made by teams of astronauts launched in Apollo capsules.

Skylab weighed about 100 tons and was built with six enormous solar cell panels. Solar cells convert sunlight into electricity, and this would power the station and all its experiments. Four panels were arranged in an X-shape on top of the telescope mount. Two much bigger panels like wings were fixed on the side of Skylab for providing power to the systems needed to keep the station habitable. Skylab was pressurized with an atmosphere of oxygen and nitrogen one-third as dense as the air we breathe on earth. The gases were kept in special tanks around the base of the station where the main engine would have been.

Skylab was launched by the first two stages of a Saturn V in May, 1973. The plan was for the station to reach orbit, open its solar panels, and prepare to receive the first visitors one day later. Things did not go according to plan. On the way up toward space, one of the two big solar panels attached to the side of Skylab tore loose in the atmosphere and came off. The second panel jammed in the folded position and would not deploy when the command was given after reaching orbit. But the worst was to come.

In orbit, temperatures reach 250° F. on the sunlit side and drop as low as –250° F. on the night side of the earth. When the solar wing tore free during launch, it carried with it insulation necessary to keep Skylab from overheating. Skylab had been launched with film for cameras, food in refrigerators, and scientific equipment on board for three separate astronaut visits. All this was damaged by excess heat. With the insulation gone, temperatures inside the orbital workshop soared to more than 120 degrees.

The first manned crew stayed on the ground and worked with engineers to find ways of saving Skylab. Together, they developed procedures to put up a makeshift umbrella over the exposed workshop in space. Ten days late, the

Skylab was launched in May 1973, but seconds after launch one of the big solar cell wings was torn free by air pressure.

Left: When the first astronaut crew reached Skylab, they flew around it in their Apollo spacecraft. One of their photographs shows the exposed hull of the workshop, heated by the sun's rays to an internal temperature of more than 120° F.

Below: The bottom section of the Skylab workshop provided areas for medical experiments, sleeping, washing, and eating.

Left: The first Skylab visitors put out a sunshade to cover the exposed hull. This shade was replaced on the second visit by a sail-like sheet, seen here covering up the first shade.

Below: Astronauts train in a Skylab simulator for conditions they will meet in space. The galley is to the left, the sleep rooms to the right.

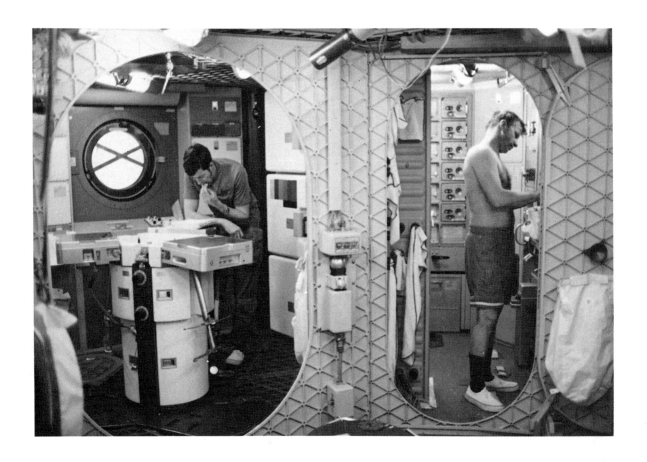

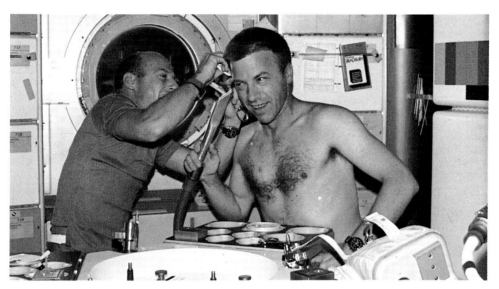

Life aboard the orbiting Skylab was made as near normal as possible. Here, astronaut Charles Conrad gives Paul Weitz a hair trim.

crew was finally launched to Skylab, where they pushed the shade out through a small, square-shaped airlock in the station wall. That did the trick, and the temperature gradually fell to 80 degrees within four days. To conserve electrical power, equipment was used sparingly. Two astronauts went outside on a spacewalk and managed to pull out the remaining Skylab solar cell wing. That restored enough power to run a reasonably normal mission.

Skylab had been built to support three teams of astronauts on separate visits. So far, the longest United States space flight had been the 14-day mission of *Gemini 7* in December, 1965. The first Skylab visit was expected to last 28 days, and the second and third 56 days each. After that Skylab would run out of air to keep the station pressurized, and food for the crew would be gone. Skylab was packed before launch with all the food, air, water, and clothing three men would need for a total of 140 days in space. Hopes of accomplishing this program had been dashed when so many things seemed to go wrong with Skylab so soon after launch.

The first mission lasted 28 days, as planned, and the crew came home. Just over a month later the second crew was launched, and with

them came a better sunshade to shield the station. They put this out during a long space walk and tied down what looked like a big sheet over the exposed hull of the workshop. The sunshade helped to lower the temperature even more. On they worked at scientific tests and medical experiments longer than originally planned. After 59 days in space, the second crew finally returned to earth.

Nearly two months after the second crew returned, the third group of astronauts went up for an extended visit. Instead of the 56-day trip set out when the Skylab program began, the third team remained aboard the station for 84 days. Scientists wanted the third crew to take pictures of a comet recently discovered and expected to be very bright. The comet would appear in January, 1974, so to capture it on film the Skylab crew would extend their stay in space. When they were launched, the third crew took additional supplies to last the extra time.

The last mission to Skylab ended when the astronauts came home in February, 1974. Since the first launch nine months before, three teams of astronauts had remained aboard Skylab for a total 171 days. Compared with the pre-launch plan of 140 days, the actual mission had been a great success, especially since many minor problems began to occur during the second and third trips. Kept working by space walks to change experiment cannisters, repair jobs inside and outside the station, and replacement items carried up by Apollo, Skylab provided a unique opportunity to watch the earth and the sun.

Above: **An important function of the Skylab space station was to take many thousands of photographs of earth using special infrared cameras.**

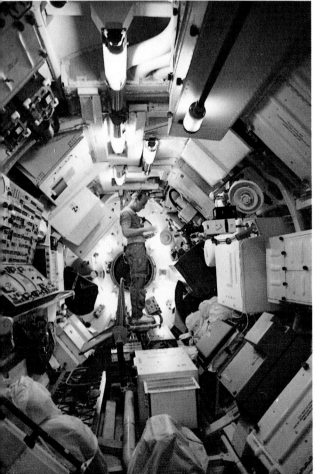

Skylab was so much bigger than any other spacecraft that it provided room for complicated medical experiments. Astronauts became test subjects for experiments to find out in detail what happens to the human body during long stays in space. Physicians wanted to know about blood conditions, how muscle deteriorates and how bone is affected. They found out about the effects that might limit the amount of time astronauts can spend in space. Other equipment was supplied by school

Left: **One module specifically built for the Skylab space station and attached to the front end was this docking adaptor, used to contain the earth-pointing cameras and the telescope control panel (left).**

Several times, Skylab astronauts had to leave their workshop and go on space walks to repair various items or to collect experiment canisters left out by a previous crew.

children in a nationwide competition for small experiments.

From Skylab, engineers learned how astronauts could perform complex repair jobs and how all the working parts of the station stood up to continuous use for nine months. Scientists gathered vast quantities of data about our sun and how it behaves. Geographers got thousands of pictures of the earth to show new mineral formations or the health of crops. From one picture, scientists were able to help famine victims in Africa find water.

15

Spacelab

Carried to space inside the reusable shuttle, Spacelab provides a shirt-sleeve working environment for scientists for up to ten days.

The Skylab space station paved the way for permanent laboratories in earth orbit. It showed that astronauts could work in space for long periods, and now NASA wanted to build a permanently manned facility. Using Skylab as a starting ground, scientists and engineers worked out the designs for a permanent space sta-tion. They watched closely how well the Skylab astronauts worked with the sleep, eating, and washing facilities. Lessons learned on Skylab were applied to the new space station and improvements made in many areas.

Before NASA could move ahead with a permanent laboratory in space, it had to find ways of cutting the cost of launching astronauts and cargo. A permanently manned space station would need supplies regularly lifted into orbit and crews changed at least every three months. Rockets capable of being used only once would be too expensive to launch. It would still be economical to launch satellites by rocket, but heavy cargo and astronauts needed a reusable space-plane.

The shuttle was the first space-plane ever built. It made its debut flight in April, 1981 and will carry cargo and people to the permanent space station NASA plans to build for the mid-1990s. Skylab was a practical use of spacecraft and rockets left over from the Apollo moon program. It pointed the way toward reusable space vehicles and permanent space stations in orbit. The shuttle was the first of the new reusable systems. It would start the process of using space for practical benefits by studying ways space can help us all on earth.

Skylab demonstrated remarkable advantages of doing certain things in a weightless state. Better components for computers and calculators can be made in space. Better materials can be made for producing miniature electronic goods. New vaccines and drugs can be prepared that promise to help combat cancer and diabetes.

Because the shuttle can return to earth with Spacelab, it can bring back many tons of valuable experiments carried out in orbit.

Skylab is carried inside the payload bay of the shuttle, linked to the forward flight deck by a tunnel, part of which can be seen assembled at top right.

Sharper views of the earth below can help farmers improve crops and fishermen find fish. In many cases, the absence of gravity helps increase the quality and purity of different materials prepared in orbit.

NASA could not afford to build the shuttle and the permanent space station at the same time. The shuttle was given priority, to prove that the means of cutting launch costs really did exist. Meanwhile, scientists could send their experiments into space using a laboratory built to

Right: Skylab comes in various configurations and can be expanded to meet the needs of the mission.

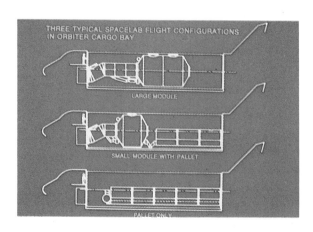

THREE TYPICAL SPACELAB FLIGHT CONFIGURATIONS IN ORBITER CARGO BAY

LARGE MODULE

SMALL MODULE WITH PALLET

PALLET ONLY

Although its primary purpose is to provide a working environment for scientists, Spacelab also consists of several pallets capable of supporting heavy experiments exposed to the vacuum of space.

fit inside the shuttle's cargo bay. This laboratory, Spacelab, was built and paid for by a group of European countries and presented to the United States. Spacelab was a valuable way of getting ready for the big station by trying out various experiments.

Spacelab is a set of pressurized modules and *pallets* capable of carrying different experiments. The pressure module is a cylinder 23 feet long and 13 feet 5 inches in diameter. It fits easily inside the spacious cargo bay of the shuttle, which is 60 feet long and 15 feet across. The pressure module lies toward the front of the shuttle, and a tunnel connects it to the crew compartment. Like railroad cars in a train, up to

three pallets can be attached to the cargo bay behind the pressure module.

Each pallet can carry up to a ton of experiments exposed to the vacuum of space. The pressure module can carry more than 5 tons of equipment in racks and cannisters inside the laboratory. Several combinations of pressure module and pallets or pallets only can be fitted in the cargo bay. A pressure module and one pallet each full of scientific equipment would weigh about 14 tons. The pallets can be used to carry very large experiments, telescopes, or instruments that need to operate in a vacuum to work properly.

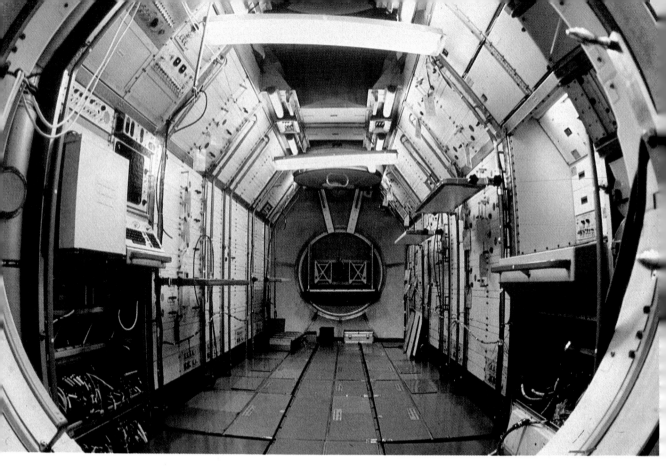

Designed like a cylindrical can, Spacelab has experiment modules that can be moved in and out as needed between missions.

The pressure module gives scientists a chance to work with their hands on experiments and equipment inside the laboratory. They can operate as they would in their laboratories on earth, carrying out detailed and complicated tests on may different experiments. Some experiments examine the way materials behave in space. Others examine the way living things respond to weightlessness. Much equipment is carried to observe the earth and stars.

The first Spacelab flight took place in November, 1983. It was piloted by veteran astronaut John Young and a fellow astronaut. Four scientists, including one European, took turns working shifts in Spacelab. The mission lasted just over 10 days and was extremely suc-

cessful. It provided a more realistic rehearsal than Skylab of how future space stations would be carried out. The second Spacelab mission went up in *Challenger* during April, 1985, carrying two monkeys, 24 rodents, and seven astronauts. It was a life science mission, although other tests were carried out as well. The flight lasted seven days.

The third flight in July, 1985, carried just three pallets and some very heavy equipment. The astronauts operated the experiments from switches and controls in the crew compartment. That mission remained in space nearly 8 days. West Germany paid for a 7-day Spacelab mission launched in October, 1985. That flight carried eight astronauts including three from Germany, the largest number of people to fly on one shuttle mission. Shuttle flights were temporarily halted when *Challenger* blew up in January, 1986. More Spacelab flights will take place from 1989 until the permanently manned space station is put up six years later.

Right: **A** European astronaut works in Spacelab gathering valuable scientific information about materials processing.

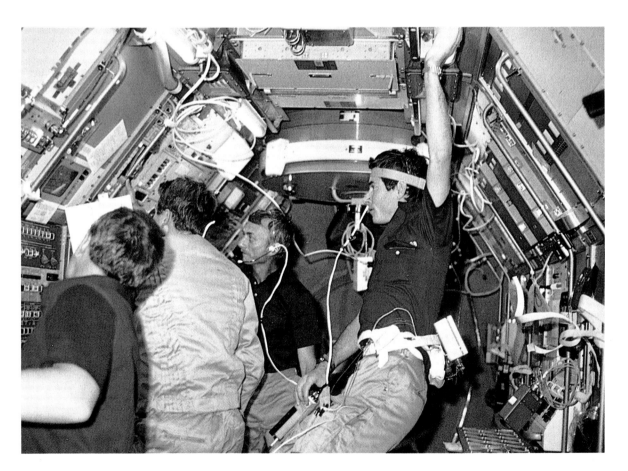

Astronauts gather around a TV monitor that reveals valuable scientific data readouts.

Designing a Workshop for Space

At first, NASA thought its permanently manned space station would look like a cylinder with docking ports for experiment modules and lavish living quarters inside.

NASA celabrated its twenty-fifth birthday on October 1, 1983. At the anniversary celebration in Washington, D.C., less than three weeks later, President Reagan said that "we're putting together a national space strategy that will establish our priorities and guide and inspire our efforts in space for the next 25 years and beyond." Just over three months later, the President announced before a packed Congress that "Tonight I am directing NASA to develop a permanently manned space station and to do it within a decade."

For a long time people imagined a space station to be the stepping stone to space travel throughout the solar system. Science fiction writers spoke of giant orbiting wheels turning slowly to make artificial gravity. Hundreds of people would live and work aboard a massive orbiting complex where space ferries brought tourists going to and from the moon or Mars. NASA does not see the station that way but does believe it to be a necessary step to colonization of other worlds.

NASA has been studying space station designs for more than 20 years. In the early 1960s, the space agency thought the best way to put up a station would be to use giant rockets. The station would be a huge cylinder with enormous solar panels to convert sunlight to electricity. Up to 12 people could live and work in it at one time. Big experiment modules would be lifted to the station by reusable space-planes and docked to each side. The modules would expand work areas and keep the main core of the station fitted out with living quarters.

When the shuttle was developed, scientists recognized that they might be able to use it for more than crew and cargo. After all, if the shuttle could lift experiment modules, why couldn't it put the station together? That way, the big booster rockets can be retired, because the shuttle will carry all the modules into space. With this idea in mind, scientists switched from rocket-launched stations to a more flexible design. They could build their station any size necessary to accommodate the work scientists

Launched by a Saturn V, the big space station was to have had large solar panels for generating electricity to power complex scientific experiments.

would do aboard an orbiting laboratory.

Spacelab was closer to how scientists envisioned the space station than Skylab, which was only a converted rocket stage. When it began flying experiments to space in 1983, the Spacelab modules helped engineers decide how to arrange the interior. Efficient workspace would be important, and people would have to have everything they needed to carry out tests aboard the station close at hand without moving too far away from their work station.

The main design challenge that the space station presents to engineers and scientists involves its basic everyday operations. Skylab was launched with all the food, clothing, air, and water the crew would need for three separate

Left: As NASA moved ahead with the shuttle, its attention turned to planning a space station capable of being lifted into orbit by this reusable spaceplane and assembled for use.

Below: Early designs of the modular space station relied heavily on astronauts, who would be able to assemble the vehicle in space from many different shuttle loads.

To boost satellites to higher orbits than the shuttle can reach, NASA is working on a space tug, which will remain at the station and carry cargo back and forth as needed.

trips. When a trip was planned that would exceed the allotted time, astronauts brought additional supplies with them. Spacelab relies on the shuttle for air and electrical power. The space station, however, will be completely independent and will have to maintain full operation everyday. It will not be shut down and evacuated, except in case of emergency.

When the President gave NASA the go-ahead to build a station in the mid-1990s, neither he nor anyone else knew exactly how it would look. The design teams had come a long way since they believed huge stations would be launched on giant rockets. During 1984, the design being favored for the station was a group of tightly clustered modules. Electrical power would be provided by solar cell panels and radiators would get rid of unwanted heat. There would be

Several designs began to evolve in the early 1980s for a permanently manned space station NASA wants to build in the next decade.

two modules for living purposes and an experiment module. A logistics module, a combined shed and pantry plugged on to the station, would house supplies brought up in the shuttle. When it was empty, another logistics module would be brought up by the shuttle and the old one removed.

By 1985, the program had changed considerably. It was to be assembled from modules built by allies of the United States. The station would be a place for international research in the peaceful use of space. In April, 1985,

Canada signed a special agreement with the United States pledging support for the station. The following month Japan signed a similar agreement, and a third agreement was signed with the European Space Agency in June.

Also in 1985, NASA decided on a design for the station. Called the *power tower,* it was to be a large structure made up from beams and trusses put together by astronauts in space. The structure took the form of a gigantic cross with modules clustered at the bottom. Halfway up would be a facility for servicing satellites with a

By 1985, the power tower design had been chosen. It had solar panels at the top and a cluster of living modules at the bottom.

robot arm. Small maneuvering vehicles would bring satellites and spacecraft for maintenance or repair.

At the top of the vertical tower, antennas would communicate with earth or other spacecraft. Lower down, the horizontal beam would carry four large solar arrays capable of producing 75 kilowatts of energy. Compared to the energy produced for satellites and spacecraft, 75 kilowatts is quite a bit. A communication satellite that relays telephone calls typically produces about 1 kilowatt of energy. A spacecraft like the shuttle produces a maximum 14 kilowatts. The power to the space station would

be split between its operational systems and experiments.

In all, the power tower design was to be 396 feet long, 294 feet wide, and 50 feet deep. Fully assembled and fitted out with scientific equipment, the station would weigh more than 230 tons. It would be lifted up piece by piece and put together over two years by astronauts working in space suits and using robot arms on the shutte and the station itself. At last NASA had a design it thought it could ask companies in the aerospace industry to build. It was not to be.

When aerospace companies began looking at the power tower design, they found room for improvements. Their improvements changed the entire arrangement of modules and trusses redesigning the station, into a *dual keel* design. The dual keel could be assembled more easily than the power tower, and it provided more space for experiments and modules.

The main reason for changing to the dual keel design was to reduce the vibration in experiment modules. NASA and scientists all around the world wanted to use the station to carry out research in materials processing. The effects of weightlessness improve the way some materials can be processed. To work properly, materials processing needs very stable conditions. When engineers looked at the power tower design, they discovered that the experiment modules would bounce around at the end of the long tower and disturb the experiments.

The dual keel design was more rigid and would give produce much less vibration. It also had a better frame on which to hang more experiments for looking at the earth and for looking out to space. Although the space station would be a place where practical experiments could be tried out, it would also be used by astronomers. The astronomers wanted to mount telescopes and special instruments facing away from earth.

Another important facility on the station would be the satellite servicing bay. That, too, had more room on the dual keel design. A flexible aspect of the new design was the way it could be added on to according to the experiment room needed at different times. It would not have to be fully assembled before the first astronauts and scientists could begin work. Instead, it could be put together over many years, rather than in one flurry of launches.

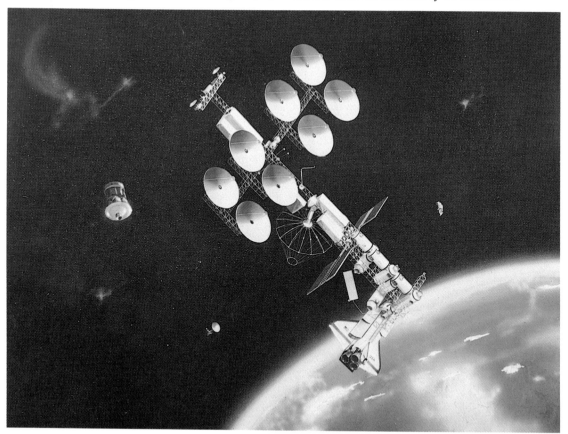

One way of generating electrical power is to focus the sun's rays onto generators that drive turbines, which produce large quantities of power.

Changed to the dual keel configuration, the NASA space station is now believed to be a more efficient arrangement of modules, equipment, and assembly trusses.

Putting It Together

The NASA space station will be assembled in space from several shuttle flights in the mid-1990s. Canada, Europe, and Japan, as well as the U.S., are all participants in the program. Together, these countries will form the first international manned space facility. The station will orbit the earth 250 miles up and contain many different sections, each built for a particular purpose. The angle of the orbit will be tipped 28 degrees.

The dual keel space station will be assembled around an open beam 309 feet long composed of trusses. The cluster of modules half way along the beam will provide living quarters for the crew and experiment modules from different countries. Electrical power will be provided by solar cell panels attached to each end of the beam. The panels resemble huge wings, and each will be up to 80 feet long. Together they will provide 75 kilowatts of electrical energy.

It will probably take about eleven shuttle flights to put this assembly into space, and the

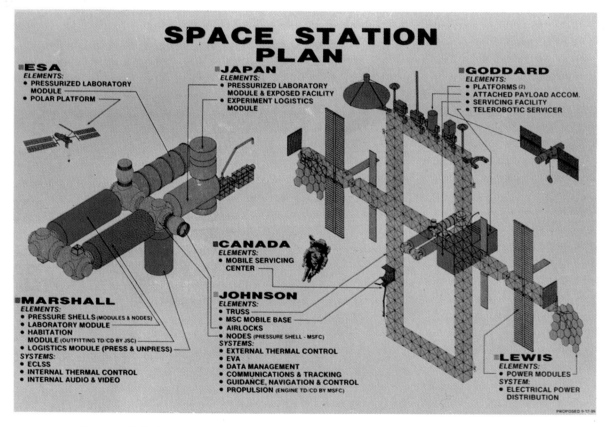

Modules built by the United States are shown in blue, by the European Space Agency in red, and by Japan in light brown. Various elements are put together by the NASA Marshall, Johnson, Lewis, and Goddard Space Flight Centers.

entire operation will probably take over a year. NASA will provide two modules 44 feet inches long, with a diameter of 14 feet, 7 inches. One, the habitation module, will be for sleeping, eating, washing, and relaxing. The experiment module will house the scientific equipment; the astronauts will work there every day. Both habitation and experiment modules each have about the same area provided by Skylab in the 1970s.

Each module will be connected to the next by a *node*. The nodes will contain equipment to keep the station running. The air, water, cooling systems, and controls will be located in the nodes. This leaves the modules free to carry equipment necessary for their particular function and prevents their being cluttered with plumbing, pipes, and control switches. NASA likes to think that a node is to the space station as an engine room is to a ship.

The two NASA modules will be attached side by side at nodes located front and back. Two other experiment modules will be provided, one by Europe and one by Japan. The European

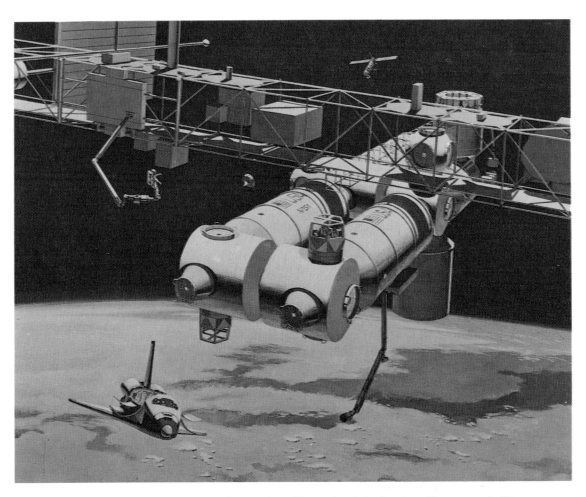

Early space station construction tasks will require bringing together several different modules and attaching a long beam or keel, to which various other systems will be fixed.

Connected by nodes, the two NASA modules to the right (one showing the crew inside) are linked to the European Space Agency module (left foreground) and the Japanese Experiment module (left background), with its logistics module on top.

module will be approximately the same size as the United States modules, with a length of almost 42 feet and a diameter of 13 feet 9 inches. The European module will be called Columbus. Built by a group of European countries, the Columbus module will be available to scientists working in materials science and in studies about the behavior of living things.

The Japanese experiment module will be a cylinder nearly 33 feet long and just over 13 feet wide. The module will be attached to a node at one end and carry an open rack structure at the other to which experiments and scientific equipment can be attached. The module will have its own robot arm for moving equipment around on the rack. Japan is also building what it calls an experiment logistics module. Basically a drum-shaped box for specimens and experiments, it is

a small cylinder 13 feet wide diameter and about 8 feet high.

The experiment logistics module will be attached on top of the large pressure module. It will be replaced every few months, when new equipment is brought up from the ground. In this way, supplies and equipment for scientific work going on aboard the module can be delivered to the Japanese using their own rockets. A maneuvering unit will collect the logistics module from some distance away and tow it to the Japanese science module. The robot arm will then position it in place. Materials being sent back to earth would go down on a scheduled shuttle flight.

NASA is providing a logistics module, too. It will be larger than the one being built by Japan for its science module. The NASA logistics

Above: Several designs for the interior of the modules have already been offered. This is a full-size mock-up of the galley and food preparation area.

Below: Assembly of the space station will be a long and complex job requiring several shuttle missions and probably lasting about two years.

An early effort will be made to provide modest satellite servicing facilities at the space station. Canada has assumed responsibility for developing the flight hardware.

module will supply all the many things the station will need to keep running at an efficient rate. As well as equipment ferried up and down in the shuttle, the main logistics module will lift food, clothing, fuel for control thrusters, and a host of minor items essential to the station's "housekeeping" jobs.

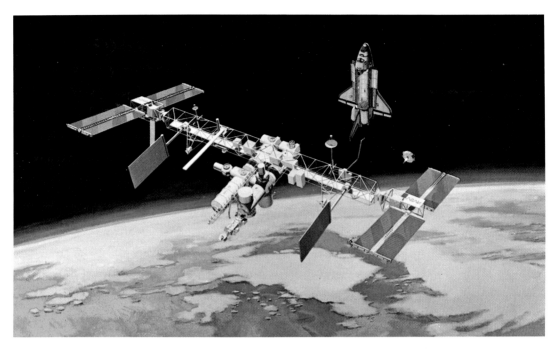

Within about two years of first assembly, the single-keel space station will complete phase one of the space station program.

Because satellite servicing is one of a space station's important tasks, Canada's contribution will be to provide two large robot arms. The arms will be used to help manipulate large pieces of equipment. They might be used to hold satellites while astronauts work on them. Some satellites break down and can be repaired. Others need pieces of equipment changed to keep them up-to-date and at peak performance. Canada is planning a major satellite servicing bay, which will form part of the station after the first phase is completed and working.

As part of the first phase of the space station, NASA plans to launch an unmanned platform into polar orbit. The platform will carry instruments for detailed study of the earth's atmosphere, land masses, and oceans. The information will be used to provide detailed mapping of the earth's resources. Unlike all the other elements, which will be sent up from Cape Canaveral in Florida, the polar platform will be launched from the west coast. Polar orbits are most suitable for observing the earth. As the planet slowly spins beneath the satellite, instruments have the opportunity to watch the entire planet.

The buildup to this level of capability will be only the first phase of preparing the space station for major scientific work. It is not precisely certain when the first phase will be complete. The launch of the first assembly mission might take place in 1995 and be completed by early 1996. Modules will be lifted up in the cargo bay, having been fitted out on the ground and packed with all the things astronauts will need to live and work in space. Other pieces, like the truss structures, will be assembled in orbit from kits flown up in the shuttle.

Different methods of assembly have already been tried out in water tanks at NASA space centers using suited astronauts. Water tanks, called neutral bouyancy simulators, give engineers a feel for how easy or difficult it will be to assemble structures in space. There is no

substitute for the real thing, however. In 1985, space walkers tried building a truss similar in design to the trusses NASA will use to assemble the main beams. In a spectacular spacewalk, astronauts proved how easy it is to put beams together in space.

With the first phase complete, the space station will consist of the NASA habitation module, one NASA experiment module, one European experiment module, one Japanese experiment module, and a small Canadian servicing facility. An unmanned platform of earth observation

Left: As the second phase proceeds, astronaut workers will begin expanding the single-keel station into a dual-keel one, with completion targeted for 1999.

Below: The fully developed dual-keel station will have a lot of extra room for complex experiments and more area for large structures like satellite servicing bays.

equipment will be in polar orbit, provided by the United States. Between six and eight people will continuously live and work aboard the station, returning to earth in shifts every three months. Everyone will live in the NASA habitation module and go to work in one or another of the three pressurized experiment modules.

The second phase of the station buildup will add a second keel. This takes the form of a huge rectangular beam structure built on to the single keel. The 309 foot beam, comprising the first phase of the station, will support the rectangular box approximately 300 feet by 125 feet. The new box assembly will frame the four pressure modules at the center of the station. It will take about a year to add the second phase of assembly to the main station. Phase two will give the station new capabilities and additional equipment.

Canada will build on the second keel a big servicing bay for satellites and maneuvering tugs designed to shunt cargo around the area of the station. Called *orbit maneuvering vehicles,* these tugs will be like harbor tugs helping to guide logistics modules delivered by rocket launchers from earth. The tugs will attach themselves to the object that needs to be moved into their proper berths and propel it around out to a distance of about 100 miles from the station. Everything that moves around in this area will be operated

By the early twenty-first century, the station may look like this, with several free-flying platforms accompanying it in orbit around earth.

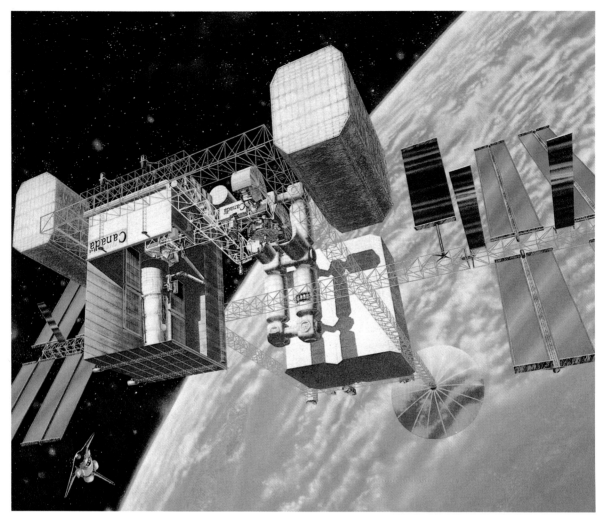

Canada will develop a fully operational satellite and space vehicle servicing facility in the second phase of the space station program.

by space traffic control. No one wants to see a big cargo module smash straight through the beams!

In the second phase, Europe hopes to launch a free-flying module similar in design to the one they built for the main station. This module will fly along with the station but some distance away. It will perform materials processing experiments free from interference with other activity on the station. Astronauts launched on the NASA shuttle, or the European spaceplane *Hermes,* will visit this module from time to time. Scientists can change experiment equipment and return to earth with samples prepared

An important vehicle attached to the station will be the Orbital Maneuvering Vehicle, capable of moving cargo up to 100 miles from the station.

automatically. In this way, they can study processes that take many months to produce results.

Also in the second phase, Europe expects to add a second polar orbit platform to accompany the one launched by the United States during the first phase. The European observation platform will carry instruments to monitor automatically the atmosphere and the surface of the earth far below. Its orbit will be coordinated with that of the United States platform, so that across fixed areas one will make observations during the morning and one during the afternoon. All this information will be transmitted to the ground. Finally, NASA will add what it calls a co-orbiting platform. Like the free-flying European science module, this, too, will not carry astronauts. It will be fitted with special instruments to watch the stars and study complex events in the universe.

Exploring the Planets

The basic space station will provide living quarters and work areas for up to eight people.

The initial buildup will begin in about 1995, and the second phase should be finished by 1999. For the first few years, people will be learning the best ways to live and work in space on a permanent basis. They must be assured that the station is capable of supporting continuous scientific activity, safely and efficiently. Then they may begin the most exciting phase of all: the exploration and colonization of the moon.

Early in the next century, a vital part of space station operations will be to act as a clearing house for samples returned from the surface of Mars, as seen here by the movement of cargo pods.

Altogether, the United States has sent twelve men to the surface of the moon. They made six trips between July, 1969, and December, 1972. What they brought back told scientists that the surface of the moon has metals and minerals that we might run short of on earth. It only makes sense that space projects should use resources available in the solar system, rather than continuing to take them from earth. The moon rocks contain chemical oxygen which, if broken down and separated, could help fuel rockets and boosters.

A space station is an ideal jumping-off point for the moon and for the planets, where so many more mineral resources can be found. The earth exerts a strong pull on objects at or near the surface. Any object must be pushed to a speed of 17,500 MPH to reach earth orbit. It takes just another 10,700 MPH to go from earth orbit to the surface of the moon. To use a space station as the starting point for expeditions to the moon would be much more efficient.

NASA hopes to develop a powerful tug to deliver and retrieve satellites to and from stationary orbit 22,000 miles out. This is where most communication satellites are situated, because at that height they appear to remain fixed over one spot on earth. Coupled together, tugs like these could provide the energy to transport men and material back and forth between the space station and the lunar surface. If oxygen could be extracted from moon rocks, it would not have to be brought up from earth.

A moon colony might begin by using space station modules similar to those attached to the

Returning to the moon sometime in the next twenty years, astronauts will unload a space station module which will form the first crude living quarters and will be partially buried beneath the surface for protection from the sun's rays.

earth orbiting station. These modules would be fitted out as living quarters and tool sheds. Because the NASA habitation module is designed to provide life-giving needs to several people at the same time, it could be used as a base on the moon. Several modules linked together would support a small scientific party.

The first moon explorers would land in small vehicles and live in habitation modules landed separately by remote control. The modules would be protected from the sun's blistering heat by special insulation. They would get electricity from large solar panels like those used on the space station. An early priority would be to put small nuclear power plants on the moon. The moon takes one month to spin once on its axis. Explorers would experience two weeks of day followed by two weeks of night. For two weeks in every month, solar cells would not be able to provide power.

As the first step, survey parties would gather scientific information at different sites for chemical analysis. The results of this analysis would tell engineers where to put the mineral extraction plants. Then the miners would arrive with heavy digging equipment to break open

As activity increases at the moon base, mining operations will extract minerals and valuable metals to help support the moon base. Some of these resources will be exported to the earth.

surface layers of material rich in aluminum and valuable metals. Soon a processing plant would be set up to separate the different soils, rocks, and metals. The waste materials would be shoveled over the modules where people lived, partly burying them with layers of moon soil. This soil would help to protect the colonists from the sun's radiation.

Left: Permanent living quarters will be buried beneath several feet of the moon's soil, as work teams come and go between the living quarters and the mines.

The aims of the first moon colonists will be to provide an independent industrial base which will be self-supporting and to develop the capability of going from there to nearby planets.

Before long, a group of 20 or 30 people would be at base camp, keeping it running smoothly. In addition, expeditions would be roaming across the surface during the two-week day. In specially protected mobile vans with huge mesh wheels, explorers would gather samples and rocks for analysis back at base during the two-week night. The camp itself would grow, and short tunnels would connect the separate modules to provide research laboratories with several different "rooms."

The moon base could be developed in the early part of the next century, and followed ten years later by the first missions to Mars. Skills learned at the moon base would aid in attempts at another dramatic venture: mining the asteroids beyond the orbit of Mars. Perhaps giant asteroids could even be towed back to the vicinity of earth, where the space station could expand to house enough workers to extract the asteroid's minerals. Whether mined in the asteroid belt or by work parties based at the space station, the materials would help expand small habitats in orbit.

Because earth will eventually run out of minerals and valuable materials, resources from the moon and the asteroids will be particularly important for people on the home planet. Perhaps several stations will orbit the earth. In time, these stations can develop into specialized work places. Some might be terminals for shuttles shunting back and forth between earth orbit and the moon base. Others could conduct exotic research in materials processing and other sciences.

Still other stations might be work rigs stationed in the middle of a cluster of asteroids, each several miles across. Gangs of workers would depart the station every few hours to dig ores. The solar system is a rich oasis of life, minerals, and materials to help us colonize worlds beyond earth and the moon. Centuries from now, the solar system may be offering us new materials unheard of today, as colonies of migrating people populate towns and villages in space.

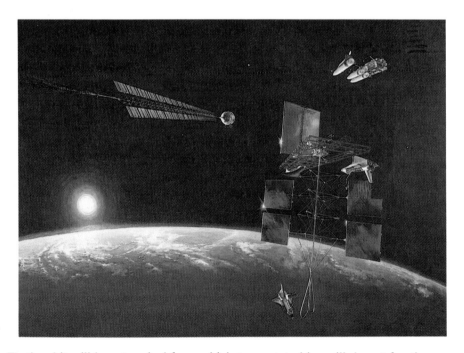

Earth orbit will be a terminal from which transport ships will depart for the moon and Mars, while shuttles fly regularly between the station and the earth's surface.

Within the next fifty years, using the space station as a jumping-off point, scientists will turn their attention to the asteroids rich storehouses of valuable minerals needed by earth and its celestial colonists.

GLOSSARY

Apollo	NASA manned spacecraft used in support of moon missions between 1968 and 1972, capable of carrying two astronauts. Also used for three Skylab flights in 1973 and for a joint docking flight with a Russian spacecraft in 1975.
Ballistic	Relates to the flight of a projectile after power has been cut off, allowing the object to move under its own momentum and the force of gravity.
Dual keel	The design chosen in 1986 for the space station, consisting of two large keels and four modules.
Gemini	The second NASA manned space program, involving spacecraft capable of carrying two astronauts. Used in 1965 and 1966, Gemini flew a total of 10 missions prior to Apollo moon flights.
Lunar module	The spacecraft used to ferry astronauts from moon orbit down to the surface and back again during the Apollo program between 1969 and 1972.
Mercury	The name of the first NASA manned spacecraft, capable of carrying one pilot, which was used to put astronauts in orbit during 1962 and 1963 for missions lasting up to 34 hours.
NASA	National Aeronautics and Space Administration, set up in October, 1958, for the peaceful exploration of space.
Neutral buoyancy Simulator	A very large water tank that allows astronauts to simulate the weightlessness of space by floating suspended in water. NASA has two simulators, one at the Marshall Spaceflight Center in Huntsville, Alabama, and one at the Johnson Spaceflight Center in Houston, Texas.
Node	A small round module with docking ports to which several experiment and living modules are attached at the space station.
Orbit Maneuvering Vehicle (OMV)	A small rocket stage normally kept at the space station used to move cargo and modules around in space.
Pallet	In the context of Spacelab, a rack capable of supporting exposed instruments and scientific equipment.
Power tower	A design chosen in 1985 for the NASA space station. It was subsequently replaced by the dual keel design concept.
Saturn V	The largest rocket built by the United States, used between 1968 and 1973 for lifting heavy Apollo spacecraft to the moon and the Skylab space station into earth orbit.
Skylab	The first NASA manned space station launched in 1973.
Shuttle	The NASA reusable spaceplane used to deliver satellites and cargo. The shuttle will carry Spacelab into orbit and back again.
Space station	A permanently manned orbiting research laboratory to be put up in the mid-1990s, capable of supporting eight astronauts at a time.
Spacelab	The European-built laboratory fixed inside the shuttle on science missions to low earth orbit, capable of continuous operation for up to ten days before return to earth.

INDEX

Page numbers in *italics* refer to photographs or illustrations.